LETTER OF CONSOLATION

LETTER OF CONSOLATION

To Comfort the Faithful
Who Endure Persecution for the Name of Jesus
and to Instruct Them How to Govern Themselves in
Times of Adversity and Prosperity
and Strengthen Them against
the Trials and Assaults of Death
Revised and Augmented

BY PIERRE VIRET

Translated from the French by Christian Fantoni

canonpress
Moscow, Idaho

The Christian Heritage Series
Published by Canon Press
P.O. Box 8729, Moscow, Idaho 83843
800.488.2034 | www.canonpress.com

Christian Fantoni, *A Letter of Consolation*
Christian Heritage Series edition copyright ©2023.
First published in 1559 in French.

Cover design by James Engerbretson
Cover illustration by Forrest Dickison
Interior design by Valerie Anne Bost and James Engerbretson
Printed in the United States of America.

Unless otherwise noted, all Bible quotations are from the 1599 Geneva Bible.

Library of Congress Cataloging-in-Publication Data forthcoming

23 24 25 26 27 28 29 30 31 32   10 9 8 7 6 5 4 3 2 1

CONTENTS

INTRODUCTION

For whosoever will save his life, shall lose it: and whosoever
shall lose his life for my sake, shall find it. For what shall it
profit a man though he should win the whole world, if he
lose his own soul. (Matt. 16:25)[1]

P ierre Viret (1511-1571) devoted his entire life to the establish-
ment of Protestantism in Europe, and he changed the world.
A giant among giants, he toiled alongside Guillaume Farel, John
Calvin, Theodore Beza, and many others to take on the mighty Roman Catholic Church, and his letters reveal the intensity of his life
and the incredible drive with which he faced adversity. Their opponents were formidable and the task at hand enormous: changing
the ways people thought and planting the Protestant Faith in the
heart of Europe. This required exceptional human beings, and Viret
was exceptional. He was a theologian who wrote many books, but
he was also a man of action, a soldier of God, and a devoted pastor.

---

1. For all the biblical passages we have used the text of the 1599 Geneva Bible.

A superstar in Switzerland, he began his ministry five years before Calvin joined him there. His reputation as a preacher was such that he was wanted everywhere: Bern, Neuchâtel, Lausanne, Geneva, all requested him. This great fighter of the Reformation was reliable. Was preaching needed? He was there. Was a theological dispute organized? He was ready. Did his sheep need their pastor? Viret met their needs tirelessly. He advised them, consoled them. He was there for them, all the time. His dedication was unsurpassed. To his persecuted brothers and sisters in France he wrote many a letter of consolation, including the one translated here. Let us follow now the footsteps of this outstanding Christian and faithful servant. Let us see him at work.

THE REFORMER

Viret lived during the early years of the Reformation. He experienced first-hand the evangelical renewal that took place in France. Born to a Roman Catholic family in Orbe, a little town in the Pays de Vaud in French-speaking Switzerland, right on the border of Lake Geneva and France, he first heard "Lutheran" ideas from his teacher, Marc Romain.[2] But it is in Paris that he converted to Protestantism while studying at the *Collège de Montaigu*. At the time, the evangelical movement was spreading rapidly in France. This spiritual revolution was spearheaded both by the *Devotio Moderna*, a new spirituality which advocated a more genuine Christian life, and by the Christian humanism of Jacques Lefèvre d'Étaples and Erasmus,

---

2. For a recent biography of Pierre Viret, see R. A. Sheats, *Pierre Viret. The Angel of the Reformation* (Zurich Publishing, 2012). For two older but important biographies, see Henri Vuilleumier, *Notre Pierre Viret* (Lausanne: Payot, 1911) and Jean Barnaud, *Pierre Viret. Sa Vie et son Oeuvre (1511-1571)* (Saint-Amans: G. Carayol, 1911). For a study on Viret's thought and theological works, see Jean-Marc Berthoud, *Pierre Viret. A Forgotten Giant of the Reformation. The Apologetics, Ethics, and Economics of the Bible* (Zurich Publishing, 2010).

which encouraged the reading and the study of the Scriptures in translation, as well as of the writings of the early Church Fathers. Guillaume Briçonnet, bishop of Meaux, adopted these new ideas and surrounded himself with evangelical preachers like Farel and Lefèvre d'Étaples. The latter published a Bible in French in 1530. The Queen of Navarre, Marguerite d'Angoulême, sister of King Francis I, was also a follower of Briçonnet. She published *The Mirror of the Christian Soul* in 1531. In the 1520s, Luther's books began to circulate in France. *The Book of True and Perfect Prayer*, printed in 1528, enjoyed tremendous success.

All these men and women were offering a new perspective on the religious life, which called for complete transformation. Thousands joined this evangelical movement. Viret was one of them. Like Calvin, who was also in Paris in those years, he was there at the right time. He went back to Switzerland in 1531 and became a pillar of the Protestant Church, and thus began a career during which he led many to the new Faith, including his own parents. It was a career that took place mostly between Geneva and Lausanne, where he became the main pastor in 1536. Through his preaching, he moved his listeners with soft-spoken, convincing, and Spirit-filled instruction. In Lausanne, he also founded the Academy, a theological school which attracted European students and scholars, including Theodore Beza who joined its faculty in 1549.[3]

Viret's influence was not limited to Switzerland. The Reformation spread throughout Europe, and together with the other reformers, he worked night and day to further the Protestant cause. This was no job for the lazy and cowardly. There was not much time

---

3. Among the students at the Lausanne Academy were five French students who were imprisoned and burned at the stake upon their return to France in 1552. For their story and Viret's support and correspondence with these students, see R. A. Sheats, *Pierre Viret*, 78-82.

to rest. This was a job for fighters, for true leaders: this was a job for Viret. He was well informed of the situation in France. With Calvin, Farel, and Beza he received almost daily news from newly arrived refugees, or by mail. The correspondence of the reformers helps us understand the political and religious climate in which they lived and the concerns they had.[4] In their letters they wrote about ecclesiastical issues, education, discipline problems, personal and family life, or the latest victims of the plague. They shared their hopes and their worries as news from all over Europe reached them and wrote about their persecuted brothers and sisters. Viret's letters are filled with compassion, encouragement, and advice.

THE SERVANT

Viret knew that the situation in France was critical for the Protestants who now had to face retaliation from the Roman Catholic Church and the State. In the early 1520s, the Faculty of Theology of the University of Paris (the Sorbonne) and the Paris Parlement united to eradicate "Lutheranism." In the 1530s, the repression of the heresy extended to the whole country. But this repression only made the reformers bolder, and they now openly rejected the doctrines of the Roman Catholic Church. As a result, many were accused of blasphemy against the Virgin Mary, the Eucharist, the saints, the images, purgatory, etc. When caught, they could face public humiliation, forced silence, intimidation, exile, imprisonment, torture, or death by burning. The times of the early Reformation were dangerous. Protestants could be arrested, assaulted and killed on the streets

---

4. For this correspondence, see Aimé Louis Herminjard, ed., *Correspondance des Réformateurs dans les Pays de Langue Française* (Geneva: H. Georg, 1866-1897), 9 vols.; see also Jules Bonnet, ed., *Letters of John Calvin* (Philadelphia: Presbyterian Board of publication, 1858), 4 vols. More recently, Michael W. Bruening, ed., *Epistolae Petri Vireti. The Previously Unedited Letters and a Register of Pierre Viret's Correspondence* (Geneva: Droz, 2012).

or in their homes at any moment. In Switzerland, Viret himself was attacked for being a Protestant pastor, but he survived. In 1533, a monk assaulted him with a knife, but he recovered from his serious wounds. In 1535, he was poisoned, but again he survived this assassination attempt. Like his fellow pastors and the thousands of European Protestants, Viret faced dangerous, deadly opposition.

But there was no stopping the conflict in France. On October 18, 1534, it culminated with the "Affair of the Placards," which was a direct attack on the Mass. For the authorities, this attack required exemplary repression. Suspects were burned at the stake. King Francis I sought to crack down on the heretics. Denunciations were encouraged. Many more Protestants were burned in the six months following the affair.[5] One of the French exiles after these events was Calvin, who met Viret in Switzerland. The two men, quickly united by a beautiful friendship and a commitment to the same cause, collaborated for the next twenty-five years.

Thanks to Calvin, French Protestantism became more organized.[6] In 1536, the first edition of his *Institution of the Christian Religion* was published in Basel, where he had found refuge with other French exiles. This book, especially after his enlarged 1541 edition, was essential to the unification of the Reformed Church. It organized the movement around a common set of doctrinal beliefs. Like Viret, Calvin did not mince words. In the Dedication to King Francis I of his *Institution of the Christian Religion*, Calvin justified the Protestant cause and denounced the injustice with which the Huguenots were treated. He was convinced that God and Truth were on their side. The Protestants were ready to die for their convictions,

---

5. On these events and the reign of Francis I, see R. J. Knecht, *Francis I* (Cambridge University Press, 1982).

6. See Ronald S. Wallace, *Calvin, Geneva, and the Reformation* (Baker Book House, 1988).

and God would give His people the ultimate victory. Here are the last lines of this Dedication, which sound like an ultimatum:

> Though you are now averse and alienated from us, and even inflamed against us, we despair not of regaining your favour, if you will only once read with calmness and composure this our confession, which we intend as our defence before your Majesty. But, on the contrary, if your ears are so preoccupied with the whispers of the malevolent, as to leave no opportunity for the accused to speak for themselves, and if those outrageous furies, with your connivance, continue to persecute with imprisonments, scourges, tortures, confiscations, and flames, we shall indeed, like sheep destined to the slaughter, be reduced to the greatest extremities. Yet shall we in patience possess our souls, and wait for the mighty hand of the Lord, which undoubtedly will in time appear, and show itself armed for the deliverance of the poor from their affliction, and for the punishment of their despisers, who now exult in such perfect security. May the Lord, the King of kings, establish your throne with righteousness, and your kingdom with equity.

King Francis did not listen. As the Reformation spread in France, persecution against the Protestants increased, especially after 1540. In 1539, the Edict of Villers-Cotterêts made it easier to prosecute Protestants by allowing secular courts to take on heresy trials in addition to ecclesiastical courts. In 1540, with the Edict of Fontainebleau, Francis I ordered all heresy cases to be handled by secular courts. The king was thus moving from a policy of tolerance to one of all-out persecution. The Edict stated that Protestantism was a heresy and constituted "high treason against God and mankind," and therefore had to be suppressed by all the force of the law. In 1551, the Edict of Fontainebleau issued by King Henry II updated legislation to condemn all manifestations of the Protestant Faith.[7]

Viret did not watch passively as his French brothers and sisters suffered. Their fight was his fight. Their wounds were his wounds. These French Protestants, who represented about 10 percent of the French population in 1560, with all the other Protestants of Europe, considered themselves the persecuted Church. They identified with the early Christians who were persecuted for their faith, just as Jesus had predicted, and considered it a blessing to be persecuted for the Truth. They were martyrs of the faith who would die in glory at the stake to meet their Lord and Savior. Jean Crespin, a printer and another refugee in Geneva, published his *Book of Martyrs* in that city in 1554, the same year John Foxe published his *Book of Martyrs* in England. The sufferings of these martyrs could not remain untold, and Viret was there to hold their hands and support them.

He rescued these persecuted men and women and welcomed them in Switzerland with open arms. Many found refuge in Geneva in the late 1540s, while others stayed in France to defend their faith at the risk of their lives. For those who decided to leave, the exodus had already begun in the 1520s, when many went to find safety and support in Strasbourg and Basel, strongholds of the Reformation. In Switzerland, the refugees were welcomed by a population and leaders who shared their faith and who wanted to spread the Gospel in France. The Company of Pastors of Geneva sent pastors to France for this purpose. More and more books were brought into the country and read by many. Year after year, the French Protestant

---

7. On the French Reformation, see Mark Greengrass, *The French Reformation* (Basil Blackwell, 1987); Barbara B. Diefendorf, *Beneath the Cross. Catholics and Huguenots in Sixteenth-Century Paris* (Oxford University Press, 1991); William Monter, *Judging the French Reformation* (Harvard University Press, 1999).

Church took shape around a common set of ideas that originated in Calvin's Geneva. Thanks to the efforts of reformers like Viret, the Protestants who had remained in France were now able to be part of congregations led by a pastor, to read and study the word of God, and to sing Psalms. These activities of course were illegal, and many were arrested and sentenced: imported pastors, students, booksellers and peddlers, and any believers suspected of heretical ideas. Despite this dangerous climate of intolerance, the Protestants held their First National Synod of the Reformed Church in Paris in May of 1559, where they adopted their confession of faith, the Gallican Confession. In 1562, the Edict of Saint Germain made it legal for Protestants to worship freely in the kingdom.[8]

THE LETTER WRITER

For those who stayed in France, again Viret offered concrete support, writing numerous letters of consolation to them. In 1559, he decided to have them published in Geneva, where he had joined Calvin. He published twenty-six letters he wrote to French believers to encourage them in their tribulations. He also composed a series of treatises meant for the French Protestants.[9] In his address to the readers of the twenty-six letters, he wrote,

> Several good people have often asked me to write letters to instruct, advise, and encourage them. These people still live in

---

8. Soon, however, the Wars of Religion started, bringing more sufferings in their wake. The Edict of Nantes of 1598 was still far away.

9. Pierre Viret, *Epistre Consolatoire* (Geneva: [Jean Rivery], 1559). See respectively, Pierre Viret, *Epistres aus fideles, pour les instruire & les admonester& exhorter touchant leur office, & pour les consoler en leurs tribulations* (Geneva: Jean Rivery, 1559); Pierre Viret, *Traittez divers pour l'instruction des fideles qui resident et conversent es lieux et pais esquels il ne leur est permis de vivre en la pureté et liberté de l'Evangile* (Geneva: Jean Rivery, 1559).

places where they cannot hear the Word of God freely. They wish to know how to live a Christian life, according to the doctrine they profess, and how to find comfort in their tribulations and persecutions. I often wrote in the past several such letters to people who requested them. These letters contain a general doctrine which can easily be applied to others, just as it applied to those for whom they were specifically written. Consequently, I was happy to allow some of them to be printed, hoping that they would be useful to some who every day need such advice, encouragement, and consolation.

By making his letters widely available through publication, Viret multiplied his influence and helped the Church grow and hope.

Initially, he probably addressed his *Letter of Consolation* to the Vaudois and the Protestants of Provence in southern France.[10] He published this letter in Geneva in 1541 in order to reach more persecuted groups as the persecutions spread to all the regions of France.[11] But the story of this letter does not stop here. Viret added material to it over the years. The result was a letter twice the size of the 1541 letter that he published separately in 1559. This is the longer letter which is translated here.

Its full title is *Letter of Consolation to Comfort the Faithful Who Endure Persecution for the Name of Jesus and to Instruct Them How to Govern Themselves in Times of Adversity and Prosperity and Strengthen Them against the Trials and Assaults of Death.* In this letter, Viret's purpose was twofold. First, he sought to encourage people in their

10. For their persecution, see R.J. Knecht, *Francis I.*; Jean Barnaud, *Pierre Viret.*
11. Pierre Viret, *Epistre Consolatoire* (Geneva: [Jean Girard], 1541). R. A. Sheats has translated this letter along with nine other letters of consolation Viret wrote. See *Letters of Comfort to the Persecuted Church.* Trans. R. A. Sheats (Psalm 78 Ministries, 2015).

difficult circumstances by telling them to remain strong in their faith and by reminding them that they were victorious in Christ. Second, he sought to give them guidance about what living a Christian life looked like. Here we see the pastor instructing his sheep from a distance. The Protestants of France, who still did not have enough pastors, no doubt appreciated this spiritual guidance from the great Viret. Here is a sample: "Do not give an opportunity to your opponents to criticize you. For if we suffer from one of our wrongdoings, there is no honor in this, but rather great shame. More than that, we gravely insult God our Father when He is blasphemed and dishonored by us. We are His children, and He should be sanctified and glorified in us." In this document, Viret does not so much lament the fate of his fellow believers as he seeks to inspire them by quoting key biblical passages to make his points. Neither does he vituperate against the enemies of God's people. The letter is filled with a peace and with the assurance that God's judgment will ultimately make things right. It is the peace and the assurance that carried the persecuted Christians yesterday. And it is the peace and the assurance that continue to carry them and to give them hope today. Let us listen to Viret now.

CHRISTIAN FANTONI

LETTER OF CONSOLATION

To Comfort the Faithful Who Endure Persecution for the Name of Jesus and to Instruct Them How to Govern Themselves in Times of Adversity and Prosperity and Strengthen Them against the Trials and Assaults of Death. Revised and Augmented. By Pierre Viret. M.D. LIX.

And now also is the axe put to the root of the trees: therefore, every tree which bringeth not forth good fruit, is hewn down, and cast into the fire (Matt. 3:10).

T o All Who Suffer Persecution for the Name of Christ, Greetings, grace, peace, and mercy from God our Father through Jesus Christ our Lord. May our good Lord, Father of all mercy and consolation (2 Cor. 1:4), bring you comfort and strength through His Holy Spirit amid the trials and afflictions of this miserable world so that you may not grow weary, but persevere with a steadfast heart in the grace to which you are called, casting the anchor of your hope onto Jesus (Heb. 6:19), who reigns in heaven at the right of the Father Almighty (Acts 1:9, 3:15, 7:55-56; Mark 16:19). For He will not allow a single hair of your head to fall to the ground without His consent (Matt. 10:29-31). He alone can do all He pleases (Ps. 114), and He wants nothing that will not serve His honor and glory and the salvation, edification, and consolation of His elect, for whom "all things work together for the best" (Rom. 8:28).

THE SUFFERINGS OF THE CHRISTIANS

Therefore, my dear brothers, since we are members of Jesus Christ, we must not be amazed or surprised if we share His cross and His afflictions. For if we desire to reign with Him (Rom. 8), we must also suffer with Him. Since He is our Head and we are His members, the Head cannot take one path and the members another. The body and all its members must necessarily follow the Head which leads and governs them (Eph. 2; Col. 1). Therefore, if our Head was crowned with thorns, we cannot be in the body of which He is the Head without feeling their sting and the pain piercing our hearts. If our King and sovereign Master, naked, bleeding, rejected, and despised was raised and hanged on the wood (Gal. 3:1), we should not expect to always sleep comfortably in this world and to receive honors and dignities, or to wear purple, velvet, and silk garments, like the wicked rich man (Luke 16:19). If we are citizens of the Kingdom of heaven, we should not expect to have all our pleasures and delights in this corrupt earth, like the children of this world. If our Lord Jesus, in his extreme afflictions, having shed all his blood, about to surrender his Spirit to God His Father, did not even have water to drink, but instead was given vinegar, gall and myrrh (Matt. 27:34; Luke 23:36; Mark 15:23), we should not be surprised if we do not have sweet and delicious wines and delicate foods every day to satisfy the pleasures of our flesh.

AFFLICTIONS AS BLESSINGS FROM GOD

What we could suffer is nothing compared to what the Lord Jesus suffered for us. Knowing the weakness of our flesh, He does not put on our shoulders a burden bigger and heavier than we can carry. For as the Apostle says: "God is faithful, which will not suffer you to be tempted above that you be able, but will even give the issue with the temptation, that ye may be able to bear it" (1 Cor. 10:13). Our heavenly Father, who took us in His safeguard and protection, knows what we need better than we do. When He brings hardships to us and gives tyrants free rein to afflict us, He does it and allows it only for our own good, so that our Faith, which is more precious than gold (1 Pet. 1:7), may be tested and refined in the furnace of tribulation, and the dross and any false metal be separated. Just like iron corrodes if it is not used, in the same way the Church and the faithful become corrupt and quickly fall asleep in this world if they are not provoked and tried by many tribulations. The flesh will always be flesh (John 3:6; Rom. 8:6). It only cares about itself. Forsaking heaven and favoring earth, it prefers worldly pleasures which will soon perish, to the celestial, eternal goods. It is therefore no wonder that the Lord wants to test and try us in many ways. He wishes to make us know ourselves as well as the evils and miseries of this world so as not to put our hearts and hopes in it, make it our paradise, and make our flesh intoxicated with it. He wants us to know that everything in it is corruptible and fleeting, that nothing is permanent, and that everything disappears like the wind and vanishes like smoke. Paul did not say without good reason that "the fashion of this world goeth away" (1 Cor. 7:31). For it is only an image and a shape that deceives those who are attracted to it. The Lord wants us to understand that human life should be called war and perpetual death rather than life (Job 13). It passes by like a shadow. Because of this, we must pursue a new life and lift our hearts to heaven. With Abraham, we should raise our eyes from the earth and look up to heaven (Heb. 11:8). For it is there that God wants us to seek a permanent and eternal city, in which there will be no change, no poverty, no misery, no tears, no weeping, no mourning, no boredom, and no sadness, but complete happiness and blessedness (Rev. 21). It is the house of God, the holy City, the celestial Jerusalem, where the Lord wipes away and dries the tears of his children and servants (Isa. 25:8), where there is no night, and where the sun always shines.

This is, my beloved brothers, the lesson we must learn in the school of persecutors and in the jails and dungeons of tyrants. There the children of God learn and benefit more than the disciples of philosophers and sophists in their assembly halls and universities. By reading the Scriptures, we learn the theory, but we shall never be good Theologians if we do not put into practice this theory of the divine letters. We shall never understand them fully if we are not tested by multiple trials. For this is how we fully understand and experience the things we read. And as we experience them, we taste the goodness, the support, the help, and the favor of God, and we realize how happy they are who trust in Him. For He never abandons them. Without this knowledge, we talk about the Holy Scriptures like untested soldiers, like those who, based on what they heard, discuss war and other subjects without any knowledge or experience whatsoever.

Therefore, my brothers, let us consider that all the afflictions and persecutions we endure in this valley of misery are great blessings from God. They teach us to mortify our flesh and to remove and replace the old man so that the new man may be more vigorous, and so that the flesh, so carnal, so proud, and so rebellious against the will of God, may learn to humble itself, obey, and be subject to the Spirit (2 Cor. 5). Do we think that God, our good Father, could be so unkind, so harsh, and so rigorous with His own children? Do we think He would have allowed His servants, the prophets, the apostles, the martyrs, even His own son Jesus Christ, the King and Ruler of all, to be thus mistreated by the wicked and the unbelievers if persecution had not been a special blessing from God? This is how we must think, though the flesh may complain, for it cannot find life in death or blessings in afflictions. Its sight is not clear enough, its eyes are not sharp enough for it to see and perceive what is outside of itself. It never sees life in any creature whatsoever. For the help and the blessings that the Lord has prepared for us are things that can only be seen by the eyes of Faith, which penetrate and pass the heavens and all creatures (Heb. 11). They contemplate and find in God what man cannot see and find in himself.

GOD OUR RESCUER

This is where Faith must display its power, where it must teach and persuade us. We already know this from experience. When we are forsaken by every creature and brought down to the very gates of hell, we feel the powerful hand of God rescue us. He makes our blood cry out, like Abel's, through whom He speaks a language that horrifies murderers, declaring that all who suffer and die for Him do not die; that even when they are defeated, they are victorious (Gen. 4:10; Matt. 23:35; Heb. 12: 24). For God works through them every day, just like He worked through Samson (Judg. 16). And so, they kill more when they die than when they lived. Their deaths are stronger and more powerful than the lives of the wicked and the condemned. For, like Cain, these remain trembling upon the earth, waiting for God's judgment (Gen. 4; Isa. 66:24). The worm of their conscience gnaws at them. They are desperate. They are at once their own executioners and murderers, like Saul, Ahithophel, and Judas before them. These are given as examples to all the tyrants, persecutors, and traitors who rise against the members of Jesus Christ (1 Sam. 31:4; 2 Sam.17:23; Matt. 27:5; Acts 1:18). We can easily understand the horror of God's judgment and the torment it brings to the conscience of the wicked; how unbearable and dreadful it is to them, as their only recourse and refuge is death, the last and best remedy they have. For if death, which according to human judgment is the most horrible and dreadful thing that can happen to man, if death is a medicine and remedy for them to escape their suffering; if they find it sweet compared to the anguish they feel, how miserable they must be since they cannot find a more pleasant remedy. For this is no remedy at all (Rev. 9:6). When they finally have it, they still cannot be at peace or delivered from hell, for they carry it within them. Rather, they enter the greatest and the deepest pits of the fury and wrath of God, which will be on their heads forever.

WE ARE NOT OF THIS WORLD

Therefore, let us not be upset if we see the wicked and the unrighteous prosper and triumph for a time while the good and faithful are oppressed, tormented, and crushed (Ps. 27). The Lord, who is an ocean of all goodness and the sovereign good of all creatures, does not want any creature to not feel some portion of this infinite goodness and experience how good He is. He does this so that His children, seeing what goodness He bestows upon his enemies headed for death, may understand by such things how gracious, gentle, and loving He will be to his friends and servants (Matt. 5). He does this also to urge sinners to repent so that by his goodness He may defeat the wickedness of men to draw them to Him and break the stubbornness of their hearts or to render them unforgivable if they persevere in their iniquities (Rom. 2).

And so, since He has prepared eternal blessings for His elect, whom He desires to reign with Him in His kingdom and live eternally, He has sent to them many afflictions in this world so that they may know that this is not their inheritance, and that He is saving for them riches that surpass understanding: riches that no eye can see, no ear hear, no mind conceive (Isa. 64; 1 Cor. 2). Conversely, He gives the wicked some happiness in this world because He does not want them to receive eternal life and celestial riches. And yet, He wants them to feel His goodness so that they may be convinced of their ungratefulness and ignorance. Consequently, He raises them in places of honor and high positions so that their fall and ruin, their shame and confusion may be greater (Ps. 37). So, we must not be jealous and envious of the goodness of God or sorry and offended if He gives to the wicked and unbelievers what He gives to the lions, the bears, the wolves, the dogs and the swine. On the contrary, we must praise Him greatly because He has elected us to inherit immortal riches. For if we put our happiness in possessions, honors, riches, pleasures, and worldly and temporary satisfactions, it would be better for us to be pigs and brute beasts rather than men. Swine only live for their own pleasure; they have their wages every day, just like any canon, monk, or man here on earth. Moreover, they are not as subject to the necessities, miseries, diseases and trouble of this world as men are. In what way, then, can tyrants glorify themselves more than brute beasts? They may vaunt their strength and power, but elephants, lions, bears and wolves are stronger. All the riches they have are produced by the earth. As for clothes, the birds and the flowers of the field have more reasons to boast. Their beauty surpasses even Solomon's splendor (Matt. 6:29). In short, the children and the carnal men of this world are the swine and the bulls of

Satan (Ps. 22:12). He fattens them to bring them to the slaughter-
house and eat them. In his kitchen, they provide the fat they took
from poor innocents.

That which the flesh admires, my friends, deserves little credit,
and that which it dreads so much is little. For the pleasures and the
adversities of this world are gone in a moment, but the evils that
worldly pleasures bring, the glory and the bliss that afflictions pro-
cure, they last forever (2 Cor. 4:17-18). The happiness of the unrighteous is short-lived and withers quickly like the grass and the flowers of the field (Isa. 40:6-8; 1 Pet. 1:24-25; James 1:10-11), but the
grief of God's children always turns to endless joy and glee (John
16:20-22; Matt 5:3-12). For this reason, it is written that they will
rejoice when the wicked weep and gnash their teeth. We must all
drink from the cup the Lord has given us, each one according to his
portion; but the wicked and the condemned will drink and swallow
the dregs, which will taste very bitter to them (Luke 6:24-26; Matt.
12; Jer. 25; Isa. 51:17).

OUR TRUST IS IN THE LORD
The Lord wants to begin His judgment in His sanctuary, in His
house; but the wicked should consider how they will appear before
Him if even the just is saved with difficulty (Ezek. 9:6; 1 Pet. 4:17).
And if this is done to green and fruitful wood, what will be done
to dry and barren wood, which is useless and only good to be cast
into the fire (Matt. 3:10; Luke 23:31; John 5)? If God did not spare
His angels, will He spare these miserable creatures (2 Pet. 2)? Let us
rejoice therefore in our tribulations. Let us rejoice of the honor He
does to us because He thought us worthy to suffer for the glory of
His name (Acts 5:41; 16:25). Let us sing praises to the Lord with
the disciples of Jesus Christ, being assured that the Lord will not
abandon us. But as He rescued Noah and his Ark from the depths

and the waters of the Flood (Gen. 7); as He rescued the children of Israel from the harsh captivity of Egypt and destroyed the evil persecutors who afflicted His people (Exod. 14), so now will He show mercy to His Church. Christ allowed the apostles' boat to be tossed and rocked by the winds, the storms, and the waves of the sea, but He did not allow it to break and sink (Matt. 8:24-26; 14:24-32; John 6:18-21). He may for a while let His Church be afflicted. He may give free rein to the fury of its persecutors and let in the winds and the storms, but when He bids them, they will cease and at once obey the voice of the Lord, who holds all things in His hand. For it is He who restrains the tyrants, like the fisherman who holds the fish on the hook. He can pull wherever he wants; the fish cannot fight back without hurting its mouth more; it cannot escape; it must go wherever it is led. For this reason, the Lord says to Sennacherib: "Because thou ragest against me, and thy tumult is come unto mine ears, therefore will I put mine hook in thy nostrils, and my bridle in thy lips, and will bring thee back again the same way thou camest (Isa. 37:29). In this same passage of Isaiah, the same tyrant and all the enemies of God and of His Church are compared to grass on rooftops that withers before it grows. The psalmist uses the same comparison to make his point (Ps. 37:2; Ps. 129:6). Therefore, if amid the depths and abysses of the sea of this world, we find ourselves surrounded by dangers and perils, we must call to the Lord as the apostles did: "Lord, save us" (Matt. 8:25). We must not look to men nor trust in them in any way. For they do not have the power to shut the winds out or to stop and calm the storms, the thunder, the swirls and the waves of the sea. God alone can, who is Lord and Master, before whom every creature trembles. He alone commands the winds, the sea, and the demons, and none can resist Him (Matt. 8:27; Mark 1:27). For this reason, we must pray incessantly so that the Lord may increase our faith, which is our victory over the world, and through which nothing is impossible to us (John 5; Matt. 17:20). It is an armor that protects the believers. They consider the swords, the fires, the threats, and all the power of the enemies of truth as chaff and dust which cannot last before the face of God, who is the consuming fire (Ps. 1:4; Isa. 57; Deut. 4:24; Heb. 2). We are terrified of the threats, chains, fetters and jails of the persecutors because our faith is lacking or too weak. Therefore, we tremble and fear. The same happens to us as happened to Peter (Matt. 14:30). Because he was worried about the winds and the waves instead of trusting Jesus, he sank into the sea as his faith failed. In our persecutions, let us follow the example of the first Christians who found their help only in the Lord, to whom they took their prayers.

This is where the believers found their help, when James, John's brother, was killed by Herod, and when Peter was jailed, waiting for death to come at any moment (Acts 12:2-4). James was killed. Peter was kept tightly in Herod's prison. The Lord kept him in that prison. Herod, that raging lion, already had his mouth wide open to devour him. But the Church was praying, and the Lord sent His angel to release him. These things are written for us so that we may be ready if it is God's will that some of us be afflicted, or even die, like Stephen and James. This is also so that we may pray to the Lord for those who are jailed, like Peter, that they may put all their trust in the Lord; that He would have pity on His poor and desolate Church. We must also pray that He give all of us a strong faith and the steadfastness to persevere to the end. For if we are imitators of the true servants of God, let us be assured that the Lord will show His power and goodness toward us, as he did toward those who came before us. If it is His will that we suffer, He will give us strength and constancy to confess His holy name. If He desires to use us, He will find a way to deliver us and snatch us from the hand of our enemies. He will send some Moses, or He will touch the heart of kings and princes, as He touched the heart of Cyrus, king of Persia, to set His people free after the great Babylonian captivity (Isa. 45:1-5; Ezra 1). Since God alone holds in His hand the heart of rulers and lords (Prov. 21:1), we must turn to Him and pray to Him eagerly (Luke 18:1; 1 Thess. 5:17). For without Him, men labor in vain. If the Lord does not keep the city, he works in vain who keeps it (Ps. 127:1). But if the Lord is at work, no one will be able to stop Him. For it is written: "The King's heart is in the hand of the Lord, as the rivers of waters: he turneth it whithersoever it pleaseth him" (Prov. 21:1).

Therefore, my dear brothers, be brave and seek the Lord's help. Accept His will gratefully. Be strong and steadfast. Do not look at the waves and the winds, but look at Jesus, who is with you in the boat. He commands and steers it, and He will not let it sink. If Herod kills the children, he will not kill Jesus, whom he seeks, and because of whom he kills the other children (Matt. 2). If he kills James, Peter will remain (Acts 12), until he dies too. And if he kills the body, he will not be able to kill the soul; and so, he will have achieved nothing (Matt. 10:28). For we should not consider him dead whose soul is still alive. The soul gives life to the body. But he is dead, he whose soul is lost until death. No one can hurt and slay the soul but us, as it appears from this cruel tyrant. He thought he had killed James, and he killed himself. For he drew God's anger upon himself. He was soon eaten by worms and lice, among which he ended his days miserably (Acts 12:23). For as he died among worms his soul was received into hell, where the worm does not die, and the fire never stops (Isa. 66:24; Mark 9:44). He who killed God's servants, who were just and innocent, is not able to die when he wants. God does not grant him the grace that he, who was the executioner of God's servants, would die by the hands of men. Rather, he has worms as executioners, which will keep eating him even after his death. They cannot wait for him to be laid in the grave and buried, but he must also see and smell his filth, and his stinking body must be the prison and sepulcher of his soul. Until his last day, he must be served by such attendants about him.

VICTORY IN CHRIST

Although Jesus was crucified and buried, death could not keep Him (Matt. 27-28; Acts 3:13-15). Likewise, the truth will not remain buried. King Sennacherib may have besieged Jerusalem after having laid waste all the land of Judah, but he could not enter the city and was defeated miserably when he thought he was winning (2 Kings 19:35-37). Pharaoh tormented Israel in Egypt but he could not keep her captive forever (Ex. 12). One day, after pursuing her, he and his army drowned in the sea, which parted before the children of God. Let us follow Moses' example: let us put our confidence in the Lord; let us not fear the Egyptians. The Lord will fight for us, and we shall see the wonders of God. Although He will not deliver us the same way He delivered the children of Israel from their captivity, He will find new ways, according to His own pleasure. We may suffer for a while, but in the end the Lord will rise and will not allow His people to perish entirely. Let us follow, therefore, our Captain and King who says: "Be of good comfort: I have overcome the world" (John 16:33). We already hold the victory in our hands. Our enemies are under our feet. They are subject to us. In fact, they cannot do anything, think anything, or say anything that may not be for our good. For "all things work together for the best unto them that love God" (Rom. 8:28). No one can hurt us but ourselves if we do not fear the one who can kill the body and the soul and put them both in the torment of fire (Matt. 10:28).

Satan seduces us and deceives us with his tricks. He is like a magician. What we think are monsters, dreadful and horrible giants, are but chaff and thorns, which the fire of God's indignation will consume instantly (Isa. 54:5-17). The Lord will also crush Satan under our feet (Rom. 16:20). Therefore, let us not be afraid and troubled since we have a Lord, a Captain, and a Father who allows, who sees, and who knows all the actions, the plans, and the plots of our enemies, whom he mocks and scorns from His high Tabernacle, which is in heaven (Ps. 2:4). To Him, they are nothing but drops of water, locusts, ants, and worms crawling over the earth (Isa. 40:17, 23-24). For without Him they cannot even breathe or move. They can only hurt His servants if He allows them to. He allowed Satan, their prince and lord, to raise his hand against Job (Job 1:12). His power is limited. Therefore, he would not dare enter a herd of swine if Christ did not allow it (Matt. 8:31-32).

So, let us consider that if the ruler of this world, the king of the children of perdition and of all the wicked and condemned, does not even have power and dominion over a swine, how little must be the power of his subjects, pages, valets and followers. For what are all the tyrants, kings, rulers and lords who persecute the truth, if not Satan's butchers, executioners, pages, and lackeys? Do they not court him? Do they not pander to him to lead souls with the Antichrist to his bawdy house? This is how they serve the Antichrist, or if they refuse to commit lechery and adultery with strange gods, they murder the poor children of God and abandon the Creator to serve the creatures. Let us prepare ourselves to die rather than forsake our Spouse, Jesus, to lust with the great whore, the mother of fornication (Rev. 17:1-2). Let us enter the furnace of Nebuchadnezzar with the Jews who entered it rather than bow to his golden statue, regardless of the beautiful music we may hear (Dan. 3). Let us throw ourselves in the lions' den with Daniel rather than stop for one day to pray, serve, and worship our God (Dan. 6).

And to get rid of our terror and fear, which by the weakness of our blind and wretched flesh we feel as soon as we hear of danger or death, let us remember often Christ's promises. Let us not stop at what we think we see with our own eyes or touch with our own hands. For Satan, our adversary, who is the master of all enchanters and sorcerers, seduces and deceives our fickle imagination by his tricks to make us believe that death is life and life death and to embrace evil rather than good. If poverty, misery, shame, infamy, dishonor, contempt, if the afflictions and torments we must endure for the name of Jesus are so harsh and difficult for us to bear, then there is no doubt that when in extreme danger, when we see our cruel and unfair death approaching, we will feel terrible pangs and we will be tested despite our steadfastness and commitment to God. If we felt otherwise, we would not be human, and our victory over the enemy and over death would not be so glorious. It is therefore no wonder that we are so anxious and troubled when we are called to this combat and assaulted on all sides. The brave soldier, or the captain, with all his courage, with all his strength, with all his valor, or with all his war experience, is also afraid when he hears the trumpet sound. For it is normal to be afraid and troubled when the time comes to confront the enemy and to charge his formidable army. Who would be so confident as not to become alarmed at the sight of weapons, pikes, and swords, when he hears the noise, and the dreadful and terrible sounds of the cannons and artillery? Who would not think that he could be struck by a thousand deaths?

A CORRUPT WORLD

We should not doubt that the poor believers, who are like sheep in the wolf's mouth, will be greatly abused (Matt. 10:16; Ps. 44:11). They will feel abandoned by all. They will receive no aid or support. A thief, a traitor, or the most despicable person on earth would be better treated. Because of this, they are terribly scared of the trials they face. The greater the trials, the greater their afflictions and torments. They believe that the heavens and the earth are angry at them. They believe that God and the whole world have declared war on them to crush and kill them. They see the kings, the rulers and the lords; they see the popes, the cardinals, the bishops, the priests and the doctors. They see the rich and the poor and people of all conditions rising against them. Some want to accuse them; others want to condemn them; still others want to kill and slaughter them. They see the torments that await them. They see the disgrace, the confusion, and the infamy they will receive before all, friends and enemies, both known and unknown. They see the gloomy, terrible, dreadful face of death. It puts a sword under their throats, a rope around their necks. It starts a fire from under their feet to bring them to a horrible death. And as they are in such anguish, as they face these trials, and as Satan has them terrified, there is no one to comfort them, to strengthen them, or to encourage them. Their relatives and friends dare not speak. They are afraid of being suspicious and of putting themselves in danger. They would, however, intervene for a thief, or a poisoner, or a ruffian, or a traitor who is their kin or their friend without being blamed for defending his cause. But when it comes to the Gospel of Jesus, when it comes to testify of the truth, its witnesses, who are the true servants of God, do not receive such support (Matt. 10). If they are brought before kings, rulers, councils and parliaments to be interrogated about their faith and doctrine, they lose all their privileges. There is no justice, no equity, no humanity, no aid for them. They are denied the rights that all divine and human laws grant to offenders and criminals. And what is worse, many times their own parents, fathers, mothers, brothers, sisters, uncles, aunts, husbands, wives, cousins, relatives, and those who should be their best friends, are the cruelest against their own blood (Matt. 10:21). Some would spare nothing to rescue someone from the gallows if he were related to them either by blood or friendship, or in some other way, and that even if he was a thief, a traitor or a criminal. But if it were for the cause of Jesus Christ, not only would they not help their own parents or friends, but they themselves would testify against them instead of trying to save them. In such cases, they are more cruel than wild beasts. Indeed, out of hatred for the Gospel, they forget their own nature and set aside all feelings of humanity (2 Tim. 3:2-9). By this we know the spirit of the accusers and of the judges who sentence them to death. We also understand the spirit of those who take such pleasure to see them tormented.

How can men be so foolish? They pity murderers and the most dangerous criminals who are the worst enemies of human society and who disturb the public peace. This peace is as essential to human flourishing as the sun, water, and fire are essential to the world. Yet a poor little sheep who could not hurt or wrong anyone, a poor child of God, for confessing and blessing his heavenly Father, is treated so inhumanely and so cruelly that he finds less help, less consolation, and less compassion among those who call themselves Christians than among Turks and brute beasts. But we should not be too surprised by this. For wolves do not eat one another and sheep do not eat wolves. Therefore, when Jesus sent His disciples, He did not tell them: "I send you like lions against bears or wolves against wolves," but "I send you as sheep in the midst of the wolves" (Matt. 10:16).

LOVE YOUR ENEMIES

Moreover, it is necessary that Jesus' members be like their commander (Rom. 8). Let us consider what kindness, what humanity Jesus displayed when He was caught like a criminal, sentenced, and crucified. Was ever robber, agitator, or traitor treated so savagely and tortured so ruthlessly, with no pity or compassion whatsoever (Matt. 26-27; Luke 21-23; John 18-19)? We must also consider that when an offender or a criminal is judged, this justice is from God and the judge who applies this justice is His instrument and minister (Rom. 13:4). Therefore, God's image must be reflected in him. God always declares His majesty, His power, and the rigor of His wrath and judgment through his ministers and servants, to whom He has given the sword (Rom. 13). All tremble when they see the courthouse. Even so, He always tempers this severity and punishment. It is impossible, even in His greatest rigor, for Him not to show a ray of His goodness and mercy. This goodness is also visible in those He appointed to represent His person in their judgments. For, as the prophet says: "In wrath remember mercy" (Hab. 3:2). But when judgment is made against the innocents, supposedly to deliver justice, the outcome is quite different. Indeed, this justice is not the justice of God. It is the justice of tyrants, which is great injustice and iniquity, disguised as justice and equity. The devil presides over this court and its judgments. Therefore, it is impossible for humanity and compassion to be present. For the devil is by nature a murderer filled with malice and cruelty (John 8:44). We cannot expect anything else from him wherever he reigns (1 John 3:8). But God is love, an ocean of goodness and kindness (1 John 4:10). That is why it is not strange that he would have pity and compassion even for the wicked. But it would be against Satan's nature to have pity and compassion for the righteous. He hates them because they are good and honorable.

Those who are justly condemned are dissolute and carnal people, but the judges, the accusers, the officers, and all the witnesses, deep down, do not feel less guilty of many great crimes than the condemned. So, we see that the world loves its children. One thief pities the other. Since they both feel guilty, they pity one another. But because the disciples of Jesus Christ are not of this world, the world does not know them (John 15:19). It cannot suffer them. It hates them and persecutes them with all its might. It looks at them in disgust, as if they were monsters. For the children of God and the children of this world, who are the children of the devil, are by nature, disposition, doctrine, life, and morals so opposite that the difference between them is bigger than the difference between men and animals (Isa. 8). They differ as angels differ from devils. It cannot be otherwise: the ones are the children of God, the others those of the devil. The children are different because their parents are different.

BE CONFIDENT

What should we do then? Must God's children suffer so miserably and die such awful deaths? Absolutely not! God's children never perish. Death itself cannot kill them. For they have the promise of the Son of God, who says: "And this is the Father's will which hath sent me, that of all which he hath given me, I should lose nothing, but should raise it up again at the last day" (John 6:39). The persecutions of God's children seem great to the flesh. But they are really nothing: just a little smoke that blurs our vision and makes us see things differently than they really are. We are like those who look through a glass: they judge the things presented to them according to the color of the glass or of the crystal they have before them. They think a thing is very wide, heavy, and big when in fact it is very narrow, light, and small. Or they believe an object is small when in fact it is large. They think it is white when really it is black or green. They see a thousand things when there is only one. An object may look like this through a glass, yet it is entirely different. For the thing remains as it is, in its natural state, even if we do not think so. The same is true about an object under water: a stick seems broken, although it is not; a penny looks as big as a shilling. Where does this opinion come from? It comes from the weakness and the infirmity of our sight, which fails to distinguish or perceive things correctly.

A similar experience happens to us when we dream, and our wild imagination controls our impressionable minds. Sometimes we fancy ourselves sitting at a banquet; sometimes we see ourselves in a position of high honor, dignity, and happiness; or we imagine that we have found a great treasure. We are overjoyed and think ourselves fortunate while our dream lasts. But this pleasure and this happiness are short-lived. They vanish with our dreaming and our sleeping. When a man awakes, all these riches and honors slip through his fingers. He is disappointed when he realizes it was only a dream. As for us, let us not cherish all the goods, honors, riches, and pleasures we could have in this world. This is not real, although we do not know it while we are asleep here on earth. Satan, the god of this world, keeps us in the dark. He keeps us slumbering so that we may not see the light (2 Cor. 3:16). But when the day of judgment comes and death is near, our eyes will be opened. We will know that all these things we thought we had and in which we placed our hopes and happiness will not profit us. On the contrary, they will hinder us. We will understand then that this was only a dream. In fact, we experience this daily when through His Word God opens our eyes to show us the vanity of this fallen world. The prophet compares the enemies of God's people who attack Mount Zion to a hungry and thirsty man who believes he is eating and drinking to his heart's content. When he wakes up, he finds that he is weary and weak, as hungry and thirsty as before. He has nothing to drink or to eat (Isa. 29:8).

What we say about riches, honors, pleasures, and delights is also true of the troubles, afflictions, dangers, and perils we face. We often believe that we have fallen into the hands of criminals who want to slash our throats; or that we are caught in a fire or immersed in water, fighting for our lives. Other horrible conceptions trouble and torment us while they last. But the man who has these dreams is safe when he awakes. He is delighted, for he is no longer assaulted by these thoughts: they are gone. When he awakes, he realizes that he is safely in bed in his house. This is how we should consider the troubles, dangers, and afflictions Satan comes up with to scare us and make us forget the Lord and renounce his Word.

But this is very difficult for the flesh. For it can only judge according to its own understanding and according to what it sees, hears, and knows (1 Cor. 2:14; Rom. 8:6). This is why we need to look to the Lord, as we have already said. We need to study His Word and find comfort in His promises. They will give us a wisdom and a knowledge which no other master, no other book can teach us. In them we shall find the remedy that will heal our deceived eyes. We will also find clearer and surer glasses to see more distinctly and judge all things more accurately. May we remember these words of our Lord and Master: "And fear ye not them which kill the body, but are not able to kill the soul: but rather fear him, which is able to destroy both soul and body in hell" (Matt. 10:28). It is already a great consolation to know that all the tyrants of the world cannot hurt us more than dogs or criminals. They can never take away our life, even if they kill us. Our days are numbered. Rather, they do us a great favor for they rescue us from the miseries and woes of this world. In return, we will find peace and begin a new life, which will be eternal.

Let us think about these words of our Lord: "For whosoever will save his life, shall lose it: and whosoever shall lose his life for my sake, shall find it. For what shall it profit a man though he should win the whole world, if he lose his own soul?" (Matt. 16:25-26). Who is so foolish who would lose his head to become emperor? Or who would want to receive a kingdom to lose his life immediately after? Christ says that the man who loves this life more than

Christ will lose both Christ and this life he loves so much. By life, He means everything that belongs to this physical life and all the pleasures of the flesh. Jesus wants us to save our soul for Him. We should not prefer this life to Him, who is our only life (John 16). Let us not be like little children who for the sake of an apple will forget the inheritance of their fathers. Let us not imitate Esau who for a stew renounced his birthright and his father's blessing (Gen. 25:30-34; Heb. 12).

Therefore, when we experience hardships such as poverty, sickness, banishment, imprisonment, or some other woe; when we feel assaulted and pressed even unto death, let us turn to Jesus Christ as to a mirror, and let us contemplate Him with the eyes of faith. May He be our refuge. May He give us strength and courage to persevere strongly and firmly in this battle. The brave champion or captain who is troubled and scared when he hears the alarm is not unworthy or cowardly. Rather he should be seen as rash and foolish if he were not. If, however, he runs away and betrays his prince and his country, then he ought to be greatly rebuked and condemned.

It is therefore not surprising if we are unnerved and worried in such dangers. But let us not consider the kind of soldiers we are, but rather who is our Captain and our Lord. If for three or four crowns a month a poor soldier risks his life for a prince who is only a mortal like him - most of the time he does not know if his quarrel is just or unjust - what should we not do for Jesus, our King, whose cause is so good and just? For He, our Captain, first gave Himself to death to deliver us from death. Let us think in what condition He was when He said: "My soul is very heavy, even unto the death" (Matt. 26:38). Let us think of his anguish and distress when drops of sweat trickled down to the ground from his body like drops of blood (Luke 22:44). He experienced horrible, unbearable, unimaginable torment and suffering. The fear of the terrible, cruel death He had to endure was more terrifying to Him than death itself. This was not so much for the punishment and pains that awaited Him, but rather for the anger and the furor of God's judgment which He had to endure for us. For it is a burden so heavy that no other creature can bear or endure it, not even the Angels who were cast into hell (2 Pet. 2:4).

CHRIST HAS PAID THE PRICE

We know that we are not Christ. We must not compare ourselves to Him. Because we are not like Him, our good celestial Father had His own Son carry this heavy burden for us. He alone can bear it (Isa. 53). Since Jesus has drunk in full the cup of God's ire and indignation, let us realize then that this drink, as bitter as we may find it, has lost much of its bitterness and has been made sweeter for us. For since Jesus has drunk it and swallowed entirely, it is no longer a cup of malediction, but a cup of salvation and benediction (Matt. 26:39). We can rejoice with David and say with him: "I will take the cup of salvation, and call upon the name of the Lord" (Ps. 116:13). For it contains no mortal drink, but it is medicine that prepares us to immortality. We see this through Jesus Christ and all his followers: through death they received life (Luke 24). Through shame, ignominy, and confusion, they came to glory and eternal bliss (Matt. 7). The path seems rugged, difficult, and unpleasant, but it leads to peace, safety, and perpetual joy. So, let us ignore the difficulty of the road. Let us look rather at those who have walked on it before us and reached the sovereign good. This good is so unfathomable that no man does, ever did, or ever will apprehend, understand, or imagine it (Isa. 64:4). For as it is written: "The things which eye hath not seen, neither ear hath heard, neither came into man's heart, are, which God hath prepared for them that love him" (1 Cor. 2:9).

Who gave such boldness to the apostles and to the martyrs? Who made them care so little for their lives? Who taught them to despise the cruel torments of tyrants? They were not Christ either. Were they not men of flesh and blood like the other men? Was not their flesh as weak and frail as ours? Who hardened them and made them so confident that no threats, no torments could scare them? They thought them no more than smoke and dust which dissipate in a moment. How many were stronger and happier in torments and death than the very tyrants and executioners who were killing them? This courage was not only seen among men who are by nature firmer and more resolute, but also among women, girls and little children. By their endurance, determination, and steadfastness they dulled the sword's blade and overcame the power and the cruelty of their tyrants (Heb. 11). How is this possible for this flesh which is so weak and sinful? Who makes it forget its nature? Who has transformed it in this way so that it is no longer flesh, so that it is able to overcome all trials and tribulations, and so that despite its weakness it breaks and defeats all human powers?

Are we to say that several apostles and martyrs were more steadfast and less fearful of torments and death than Jesus Christ? For we do not read that any man, no matter the cause of his suffering and the pain he was expecting or endured, was ever so anguished that out of distress and horror he sweat blood. Or if such a thing did happen, it happened so rarely and so secretly that no accounts exist. Should we say then that Christ, the Head of all God's children, the Holy of holies, the Perfect of perfects, was more imperfect, more timorous, weaker, more fearful, and less steadfast than the poor sinners for whom He suffered? We would be insulting our Savior if we said this. We must consider instead the causes of his great distress. We must think about why we, the evangelical saints, tell these things so faithfully and with so many details.

First, He clearly wanted to show that He was truly man and that He suffered like a normal man; that He had the same body and soul we have and that He shared our common flesh and blood. He was in every way like us, except that He was sinless (Eph. 5:2; Heb. 2:9-11, 4:15). For if He was not a real man, we could not have assurance of our salvation or comfort in our troubles. We find them from Him, in Him, and by Him. He also tells us how He was afflicted in His flesh, overwhelmed by the judgment of God, which He bore for us. He really went into hell and felt our damnation in Himself, a damnation we had deserved and earned (Isa. 53). He was despised and abandoned by God (Ps.22). He really felt the pains of hell, the anger, the wrath, and the vengeance of God because of our iniquities and transgressions, which deserved death and eternal damnation. So, we should not lose heart. What happened to Christ should help us overcome our infirmity and our weak flesh. Nothing should make us stronger and encourage us more to despise dangers and to risk our lives for the glory of God. Why was Christ so anguished? He was so scared of hell that the Angels came to comfort Him (Luke 22:43). This happened so that we may know and believe that He bore God's anger and judgment for us (Isa. 53). Our flesh was punished for its sins in Him and in Him endured what it deserved so that it may not have to carry by itself all the burden of God's wrath and indignation. Instead, it is delivered from it and saved. Malediction was changed into salvation by Him who was hanged on the cross and cursed for our sake (Gal. 3). Why did He want to be forsaken and deprived of all help, assistance, comfort, and consolation? It was so that we may never be forsaken or abandoned by God, but rather received in His provision and protection. He delivered us from all evils. Why did He want to drink the cup and such a bitter drink prepared by the Father if not to make it sweeter for us? For if we had to suffer such a judgment from God, which we deserve, and swallow the full cup of His wrath, not even one of us, however godly, would be spared. On the contrary, we would all be consumed by death and eternal damnation.

Since Jesus has converted the curse into a blessing; since the cross, the afflictions, and death lead us to salvation, they are not to be feared. For the great horror and torment of the cross we must carry does not come so much from the pains we suffer as from the knowledge of the wrath and judgment of God. We think that God is angry at us and has totally abandoned and rejected us. For since Satan, our chief and mortal enemy, seeks to destroy and ruin us, he is constantly looking for the best ways and occasions to achieve this goal. For this reason, Peter compares him rightly to a roaring lion on the prowl (1 Pet. 5:8).

BE ON YOUR GUARD AGAINST SATAN

No other occasion is better for him than when a man is afflicted and struck by the hand of God. This is when he uses all his power, all his zeal, and all his tricks to divert him from trusting God and convince him that God hates him and has forgotten him; that He wants to destroy and ruin him. He uses current woes and afflictions as sure proofs and obvious evidence. To the blind and ignorant flesh, they seem to be undeniable signs and proofs of God's displeasure and wrath. Satan knows the flesh. He takes advantage of it and tries to maintain it any way he can in this distorted and bad opinion of God. For he knows that if a man keeps his trust and hope in God, he will not be able to harm him. That is why he uses all his power to deprive him of his faith, or at least to weaken it, so that it may not be able to resist him. He knows that when he has achieved this, a man will be helpless and disarmed and will surrender to him. He could never accomplish this if a man stood firmly in his faith. The fiend is like a crafty enemy. He looks for all possible means to achieve his task. He pounces on the poor sinner when he is weakest and most troubled. He assaults him on all sides to surprise him more easily, and as he closes in, his victim does not know which way to turn. He makes him stumble and pushes him to blaspheme against God.

Therefore, we should follow the apostle's advice to us concerning this dangerous adversary: "Whom resist steadfast in the faith" (1 Pet. 5:9) and "Be sober, and watch" (1 Pet. 5:8). Let us say with him as well: "And lead us not into temptation, but deliver us from evil" (Matt. 6:13; Luke 11:4); "Lord, increase our faith and do not forsake us" (Luke. 17:5). For this war which Satan wages against us is our biggest battle (1 John 5). It is a most dangerous path (Eph. 6). If we manage to overcome these trials and, with the shield of faith, stop the burning arrows of the old serpent, our ancient fiend, we shall easily overcome everything else. For if we find refuge in the wounds of Jesus and are convinced through Him that God is a gracious, kind, and supportive Father to us, then our victory is complete. No sin, no death, no hell, no devil may afflict us; no pain or torment may be too hard to bear. But without this assurance and belief, there is no little trial, no little pain that will not be difficult for us to endure. For our lack of faith is the main cause of our fears and troubles. It is the reason why we are deceived in the first place, why we imagine these false conceptions of God. They harrow us. Without them, our afflictions would seem very light.

We see this in those who have been forsaken by God. They find no comfort in Him because they have no faith in Him. For why did Cain suffer so much? Why was he afraid to be killed (Gen. 4)? Why did he tremble when a single leaf was stirred by the wind? Did he fear he would be placed on the execution wheel? Did he fear his limbs would be crushed and broken? Did he think he would be hanged ignominiously on the gallows? Who jailed him and brought him to the executioner? Why was he afraid he was being followed? The Scriptures mention no other human beings on earth other than his father and mother. They were not seeking his death. Besides, he was the master and the lord of those who were born of him and who multiplied on the land of his race. He had no physical pain. Yet he suffered much. What caused such great anguish, such fright and unbearable torment? It was the horror of God's judgment and the testimony of his guilty conscience. They gave him no rest. They pursued him more ruthlessly than a tyrant.

We can say the same about Judas. Who forced him to put a rope around his neck (Matt. 27:5; Acts 1:18)? Did Pilate condemn him to die as he did Christ? Did the scribes, the Pharisees, the Sanhedrin, and the people of Jerusalem persecute him, hand him over to Pilate, and bring him to the executioners? He was their good friend, well-liked by all. Instead of pursuing him, they would have protected him if someone had wanted to punish him for his act. And yet we see what happened to this lost man who enjoyed the favor of the world. Although he was not threatened by anyone, he did to himself something worse than any enemy or executioner could have done to him. He felt great distress, great sorrow, and torment. But where were his tormentors? He was his own tormentor. For as the prophet says: "But the wicked are like the raging sea, that cannot rest, whose waters cast up mire and dirt" (Isa. 57:20).

We must conclude that our sufferings, pangs, and afflictions do not come directly from the woes we endure, but chiefly from the fear of the wrath and judgment of God. But since Jesus Christ has borne it for us, our pain is much less. It is lighter, and our condition is different from the condition of the wicked and of the reprobate. For they are greatly tormented, even when they prosper, without being persecuted by anyone. But God's children, even when they are persecuted by the fires of their enemies, have joy and suffer less than their tormentors. And who is the cause of this difference if not Jesus Christ who endured the wrath of God for his members (Rom. 5)? Thereby, being assured of God's grace and mercy, they are so comforted that their sufferings are nothing to them. For they know that they have been reconciled to God, who does not send such afflictions to destroy them, but to save them. The wicked, on the contrary, who have no part in Jesus Christ, must carry the burden of God's wrath and drink the cup of his anger (John 3:18; Isa. 51:17).

CHRIST OUR SAVIOR

Therefore, when we are attacked, let us look to Christ, who was afflicted for us even unto death. Let us remember His sweat when He was in agony. Let us listen to Him: "O my father, if it is possible, let this cup pass from me: nevertheless, not as I will, but as thou wilt" (Matt. 26:39). Let us hear His voice when He was on the cross, fearing hell: "My God, my God, why hast thou forsaken me" (Matt. 27:46; Ps. 22:1)? By undergoing death and God's wrath and indignation, He has overcome all things (Heb. 4; 10:9). He has leveled out and prepared the way for us, and He has removed our fears. Since He has endured such thorns; since He is our brother, made of our flesh, blood and bones, He who has experienced our infirmities and was tempted in all things, more than any other creature (Heb. 2, 4, 5; Eph. 5), He will have pity and compassion for us. He will deliver us from our affliction, as He delivered Himself from it (Rom. 4; Acts. 1; 1 Cor. 15). We know that He is not dead, but that He rose from the dead, went up to heaven to take possession of it and of the Kingdom of God, for all of us, of whom He is the Head (Eph. 2; Col. 1). Let us be assured that as we suffer and die like Him, we will receive His glory and resurrection (Rom. 8).

He did what He did, not for Himself, but for us. Since He overcame sin, death, hell, and Satan, we can say with the prophet and with the apostle: "O death, where is thy sting? O grave, where is thy victory?" (Hos. 13:14; 1 Cor. 15:55). Who will accuse God's children (Rom. 8:33)? For since He is our Father and we have His Son Jesus Christ as our intercessor and advocate, who is seated to his right and intercedes continually for us, whom shall we fear? (1 Tim. 2:5; 1 John 2:1). "Who shall separate us from the love of Christ? Shall tribulation or anguish, or persecution, or famine, or nakedness, or peril, or sword" (Rom. 8:35)? Will a thing past, present or future? Anything? Will the heavens or the earth, fire or water, or any creature? Nothing will separate us from the love of God poured into our hearts through Jesus Christ. If we find it difficult and disturbing to leave this world, our families and friends, our goods, our lands and possessions, our pleasures, our honors and joys, let us think of what we are exchanging them for (Matt. 19: 29; 10). Let us consider the great difference between what we leave behind and what we shall gain. What do we lose in leaving this miserable world where all things are corruptible? We are changing corruption for incorruption, mortality for immortality, poverty for riches, confusion for glory, honors for honor, sickness for health, prison for liberty, tyranny for reign, death for life (1 Cor. 15)? What regrets shall we have to be separated from this horrible world? Who shall we be separated from? From wicked and detestable sinners. To what end? Is it not to be among the Angels, the firstborn, the perfect spirits? Is it not to be on holy Mount Zion and in the celestial Jerusalem, the city of God and true Republic of all the elect, in which God alone forever reigns in perfect goodness and happiness (Heb. 12:22-24; Rev. 21)? Are we afraid to reach this happiness for which we were born, which we all seek, and in which we shall find our perfect fulfillment?

WE HAVE ETERNAL LIFE

Socrates was a poor pagan who had never heard God's Law or the doctrine of the prophets and the apostles. He was entirely ignorant of the Holy Scriptures and had no promise or assurance of eternal

life. Yet they say that he rejoiced at the prospect of death because
he believed and hoped that he would see and talk with Homer and
other great people who had died before him. If this pagan man
found comfort and joy at his death in this hope, what joy should be
ours at the sure hope we have in heaven? Socrates only had his opinion as to what was to come. And even if he had found everything
he expected, what was that compared to what we are sure awaits us?
Will God not condemn us, after so many testimonies of the Law, of
the prophets, of Jesus Christ, of his apostles, and of his disciples and
martyrs? Will he not condemn us if after so many signs, after Christ
died, rose again and ascended to heaven, we still doubt eternal life
and are sorry to leave this miserable world, this valley of misery, to
go to rest in the house of our father? Shall we be sorry to go to Jesus
our Savior to enjoy the blessed, eternal life He gave us, to reign with
Him and with all His angels and blessed spirits?

History books contain many examples of non-Christian nations
who commonly practiced suicide to avoid disgrace and dishonor or
submission to their enemies. Do we care more about this mortal
life than these poor pagans who were blind and ignorant? They had
no certainty or firm hope of another life. But we have promises of
not only the immortality of our souls, but also of the resurrection
and immortality of our bodies, and of eternal life. They preferred to
kill themselves brutally than live in dishonor under the yoke and
servitude of other men. Do we prefer to live in impurity? Shall we
blaspheme Christ, carry the yoke of the Antichrist and suffer the
harsh tyranny of the devil rather than follow Jesus, our Savior and
Captain, and go where He calls us? He asks nothing of us that He
did not do first to ease our path.

LIVE A CHRISTIAN LIFE

He does not tell us to end our days. For this is no proof of courage, as the pagans thought. It shows weakness and despair. All He asks from us is that when He calls us and our time has come, we show the faith and the hope we have in Him; that we value His glory more than our own life (Matt. 10:39). He does not want us to throw ourselves rashly into danger and die without a good cause. But He does require of us that we do not blaspheme against Him in order to escape and avoid death when He sends it to us. He wants us to always be ready to follow His good will (Job 14:15). For we know that our days are numbered. He has put a limit on our lives (2 Pet. 1:14; Isa. 38:5). He has placed our souls in this earthly and fallen body as in a tabernacle. It has no firm footing. It will change and change again, and move from one place to another, until we reach the end of this terrestrial journey. Our soul is in our body as in a garrison. It must stay and protect it until her Emperor, her King, and her Lord who put her there, calls her back. Until he is released by his Commander, regardless of the hardships, troubles, or dangers he may face, a good and loyal Captain or soldier cannot leave the place he was asked to defend. Similarly, until God has ordained it, a man may not take his life, which God has given him, or seek death because of the evils and troubles he encounters. God made us, and He will unmake us and make us again, according to His good pleasure. He does not want us to desire death or to fear it, but if we do, it should be how God's true servants feared and desired it. If they sought death, like Elijah (1 Kings 19), they did not do so out of impatience or despair for the troubles and vexations they suffered on earth, but because they could not bear men's blasphemies and insults against God. If they desired life, it was not because of all the pleasures of the world. It was for God's glory. For they feared that after they died, He would be dishonored. They feared that the wicked would blaspheme against Him. They felt as if God had removed them from this world, as He removed the wicked. David, Hezekiah (Isaiah 38), and several others were like this. When they knew that their life or their death could be used for God's glory, they were ready for either one, as Paul testifies about himself. As for himself and his own benefit, he had more reasons to want to be delivered from this mortal body and be with Jesus Christ than live any longer among the sufferings and evils of this world. But, knowing that his ministry was still necessary to the Church, he happily endured and suffered all the hardships God sent to him (Phil.1 21-26). And although he knew the places that were being prepared for him in Jerusalem, while he was still free, nevertheless being assured by the Spirit of God that they would serve for God's glory and honor, he was not only ready to endure the chains and shackles, but also to expose his blood and his life for Jesus Christ (Acts 20-21). Let us therefore imitate this godly apostle. Let us remember often Jesus' words: "He that heareth my word, and believeth him that sent me, hath everlasting life, and shall not come into condemnation, but hath passed from death unto life" (John 5:24). And the time will come when those who are dead in monuments and sepulchers will hear the voice of the Son of God and will rise again: some to eternal life, others to perpetual damnation.

We have good reasons to despise death, to face it bravely, and to no longer fear it. They are not found in the books of philosophers, although they tried hard to convince men of the immortality of the soul. Theirs were only human reasons, some of which were very weak and irrelevant. They could not strengthen and comfort the conscience when death came. Still, we read in history books that pagans used these reasons to brace themselves against death and face it more firmly. They say that the night Cato of Utica decided to take his life to escape Caesar, someone was reading Plato's book on the immortality of the soul to him. And yet Julius Caesar would have gladly spared his life, and considered it a great honor to do so. It was written also of Cleombrotus that after reading this same book he was so convinced of the immortality of the soul that, although he never suffered any troubles, hardships or adversities, he jumped from a wall into the sea, thinking he was leaving behind a miserable life for a happy one (Saint Augustine, *City of God*: I, 22; Cicero, *Tusculan Disputations*, LIX).

We should be ashamed if we did not give more credit to the Word of God, which is the infallible truth, than to the reasons of a mortal man, blind, and ignorant of what he writes about an act that goes against God's will. Other miserable idolaters like this man believe these reasons too. We would greatly wrong Jesus Christ, our great celestial Doctor (Matt. 23:8-10) and sovereign Master, who has told us about life after death on so many occasions. He did it first in His predications, then by his many signs and miracles, and finally by His death and resurrection and the testimony of so many prophets, apostles and martyrs who did not hesitate to die. Some Romans and Athenians decided to put an end to their own lives. They did so not so much to serve as examples, although that was an important consideration. They did so mostly for glory and immortality. It would be a great shame if we could not find any Christians who would be more fervent and who would not give their lives for the honor and glory of God, for the edification of his Church, and for the good and salvation of all the Christians. For this is the way to gain true immortality.

Blessed is the man who is led by the Holy Spirit to give his life. On the contrary, miserable is the man who has neither faith nor hope. He is always afraid. Indeed, he is more dead than alive. He suffers more in living than the others in dying. Let us therefore cast this fear far away from us and let us call upon the Lord. And our

God, who delivered the three Hebrews from Nebuchadnezzar's fiery furnace (Dan. 3), who rescued Daniel from the lions' den (Dan. 6), who resurrected His Son Jesus Christ, and helped all His servants (Heb. 13:6-7; Josh. 1:5), our God will not forsake us. He will deliver us from death and danger if we also trust in Him alone. And whatever befalls us, we will write as Paul wrote to the Corinthians, saying: "For brethren, we would not have you ignorant of our affliction, which came unto us in Asia, how we were pressed out of measure passing strength, so that we altogether doubted even of life. Yea, we received the sentence of death in ourselves, because we should not rest in ourselves, but in God, which raised the dead. Who delivered us from so great a death, and doth deliver us: in whom we trust, that yet hereafter he will deliver us. So that ye labor together in prayer for us, that for the gift bestowed upon us for many, thanks may be given by many persons for us" (2 Cor. 1:8-11).

But above all, let us not provoke Him (Deut. 6; Matt. 4). Let us not put our trust in men only. The Prophet says: "Put not your trust in princes, nor in the son of man, for there is no help in him" (Ps. 146:3). But as Jeremiah says: "Cursed be the man that trusteth in man, and maketh flesh his arm, and withdraweth his heart from the Lord. For he shall be like the heath in the wilderness, and shall not see when any good cometh, but shall inhabit the parched places in the wilderness, in a salt land, and not inhabited. Blessed be the man that trusteth in the Lord, and whose hope the Lord is" (Jer. 17:5). "He shall be like a tree planted by the rivers of waters, that will bring forth her fruits in due season: whose leaf shall not fade" (Ps. 1:3). We are at war with Satan, with the rulers of this age, and with the rulers of darkness. Therefore, we need a power more than human to put our enemy to flight, ruin and overthrow him (Eph. 6). We and our enemy fight with our own arms. Like us, he has swords and armors. And while flesh fights against flesh, man against man, victory will always be uncertain, hard-fought and dangerous for both. In the end, one will overcome the other. But if the Spirit descends onto the battlefield and fights against the flesh, if a man goes to battle armed with the arm of God, clothed with the valor from above, all human armies will tremble before him. The camp and the army of the prince of this world will swiftly be defeated, as we can see with David (1 Sam. 17). For by himself he defeated the giant Goliath and cut his throat. A child, a shepherd, without any weapons other than a sling, brought down the terrifying giant who had been trained for war all his life. He was heavily armed and equipped, he who terrified Saul, the King of Israel, and his entire army. When David put on his armor, he could not walk. But when he took it off, he attacked the conceited and formidable giant who despised and mocked him, and the Lord put such power in David's sling that he brought down Goliath. The latter supplied him with the very weapons and the knife to cut his throat.

This is what happens to us every day. When we put our trust in men, in their judgments, power, and strength, we can do no good. But when we trust God alone, the more desperate our circumstances seem to our human understanding, the more powerful we are, and we see God's great wonders. On the contrary, when we seem to have more help, more relief, and more assistance from men, we achieve less. Everything we think we hold slips through our hands. Our plans and undertakings fall apart. Why is that? The main reason is that when life is good, when we feel strong and safe, we rely less on God. Our trust and hope are divided. Instead of looking up to God alone and resting upon Him only, we rely on our own forces and abilities more often than we rely on God. We do not even notice it. We think so highly of ourselves that we are deceived. We hide our infidelity and hypocrisy behind a beautiful show. Our eyes are fooled. This causes much suffering. The stronger we think we are, the weaker we are. This is when we are most helpless. For we are hampered by the weapons we trust. These weapons impeded David also. Like David, we must cast away the weapons of Saul the proud. Instead, we must pick up stones from the brook, and armed with the power of God, we must wait for our enemy and attack him.

THE APOSTLES . . .

The apostles had no emperors, kings, rulers or lords to help or protect them. All were against them. All power, riches, authority, dignity, excellence, knowledge and human appearance stood against them. They were like an indestructible and impregnable tower or bastion, in which all the might of the prince of this world had gathered. But the apostles were armed and equipped with the guns and artillery of the real and living faith. They bombarded their enemies with the cannonballs and the stones of their prayers. These prayers were loaded with the power of their faith. They burned with the celestial fire that consumed their hearts. It is more powerful than any human-made fire or powder used for artillery. This is the fire they used to bring down the mighty towers that rose against God. This is the fire they used to capture all human thoughts and bring them in obedience to faith (1 Cor. 11). With it they shook the whole earth. They knocked down castles, fortresses, and prisons (Acts, 4:31; 12:7; 16:27). They opened and broke doors, chains and shackles. They confronted their enemies head-on. They opposed the efforts, the plans, the machinations, and the ruses of Satan and his followers. Despite these enemies, this leaven of the Gospel of Jesus Christ has caused the dough to rise greatly. This little mustard seed has grown so much that its branches have extended to the whole world.

...AND US!

Today there are so many of us. We are supported by so many powerful people, Princes, Lords, and Republics. And yet we are not active enough. We are moving backward rather than forward. Instead of getting hotter, we are getting colder. We are not just tepid. We are ice-cold. This is happening to us because we are misplacing our trust. We rely on men, who are nothing but shadows and smoke. They disappear and vanish before our very eyes (Job 1). We lean on the reed of Egypt, which is weak and fragile. It cannot support such a heavy burden, and so it snaps and breaks in our hands. It makes us fall. Its splinters wound and bruise our hands. This would never happen to us if we rested on the solid rock which no wind, rain, or storm can move or shake (Isa. 8; Matt. 9). We say with the prophet: "They that trust in the Lord, shall be as mount Zion, which cannot be removed, but remaineth forever" (Ps. 125:1); "The Lord is my light and my salvation, whom shall I fear?" (Ps. 27:1); "The Lord is my rock, and my fortress, and he that delivereth me, my God and my strength: in him will I trust, my shield, the horn also of my salvation, and my refuge" (Ps. 18:2). "I will not fear what man can do unto me" (Ps. 118:6). "Though my father and my mother should forsake me, yet the Lord will gather me up" (Ps. 27:10). For everything that happens to us has gone through the immutable council of God. Just as His essence is unchangeable, so is His providence (Mal. 3:6; Isa. 14; 40). Therefore, we should humble ourselves before Him and submit ourselves to His will.

While the children of Israel were in Egypt, they were held in the harsh captivity described in the Scriptures. The great cruelty of the tyrants who held them captive was like a furnace of iron. They received no help, no protection, no assistance, no assurance from any rulers or peoples on earth (Deut. 4; 2 Kings 8). Since they were deprived of any human aid or protection, they cried out to God, as a child cries out to his father. This helped them more than any human aid, support, or protection. For when cruelty was greatest; when it had reached its highest level; when the situation was desperate, God extended His mighty hand with which He delivered His own people. This was not done with a human arm. No tyranny is eternal. When a bow is bent too long, it will break. The more bent it is, the likelier it is to break. Nothing can overcome the violence of tyrants but the endurance of the saints. Nothing can dull the blades of their swords; nothing can diminish and extinguish their fires but faith and constant prayers.

GIVE GOD THE GLORY

My dear and beloved brothers, I say this so that you may not test God or look down on the means He gives us and wants us to use. For ignoring and rejecting these God-given means and opportunities would not be acting in faith. Rather, it would be testing God. He is the One doing the work. The instrument He uses and holds in His hand does not do the work. This is not to say that we should despise the instrument. But we should not look so much at the instruments as we should look at Him who provides them and uses them. We often fail to do this. We look at the saw and the ax that cut, but we fail to lift our eyes to the One who holds them in His hand and makes them cut (Isa. 10:15). The master and the laborer complain when their servants, their apprentices, and the instruments they use get the credit instead of them to whom credit is due. For God said: "I am the Lord, this is my Name, and my glory will I not give to another, neither my praise to graven images" (Isa. 42:8). Generally, the more masters there are, the worse is the work. The Lord manages His own matters perfectly. Sometimes He does not want any helpers so that He, not them, may receive the glory for the work done. We can see this in Gideon's victory over the Midianites (Judg. 7). The Lord, the great Captain only wanted three hundred men to fight His enemies, even though their multitude looked like ants and locusts covering the entire land. Why did He turn down so many soldiers and give the victory to this small number He kept? He Himself gives the reason: He did this so that the Israelites might not attribute the honor and glory of this great victory to their own strength and weapons, but to the hand of God. Yet Gideon, as a prudent and courageous captain, did not neglect any of the duties God had entrusted him. He did not go to bed and fall asleep waiting for God to deliver his enemies into his hands. He prepared himself as best he could, as if to obtain the victory through his own labor and industry. He did all this without trusting in his own work and strength. He did not use any wicked or unjust ways. He just used the way God had recommended him. His hope of victory laid in Him alone.

For this reason, let us seek the means God supplies for us. Let us use them and not test Him by rejecting Him for His creatures. Let us use the creatures in such a way that the creator may not be offended. May our hearts not trust them completely or even in part. May we not look at the rod, but at the One who holds it. May we not only look at those who are God's instruments to serve us. Let us not consider the soldiers, but the Ruler they serve, the Captain who leads them. Let us fight against the Amalekites (Exod. 17) alongside the children of Israel with the weapons God has provided for us. But let us also be assured that we will not be able to conquer our enemies without the help of our great Moses, that is, Jesus Christ, who intercedes for us on the highest mountain. He stretched His arms, lifted His hands on the cross to help us win the battle, and give us victory over all our enemies (Rom. 8). During this victory, we will feel a wonderful assistance from the Lord, an assistance we could never have imagined.

BE HOLY

Let us remember the Lord's admonitions: "By your patience possess your souls" (Luke 21:21) and "Be ye therefore wise as serpents, and harmless as doves" (Matt. 10:16). Be wise, but be careful that you do not use your wisdom for deceit and evil. Be harmless in such a way that your harmlessness does not become foolishness. This would be an offense to God's Word. Trust in God, but make sure that your faith and your trust are firmly grounded in the Holy Scriptures in order to avoid temerity and error. Be zealous in the work of the Lord. Pursue it with a fervor that will not be made cold by the wisdom of the flesh. May it not turn into rage or fury, but rather be tempered with understanding and Christian moderation. Confess Christ in all places and situations (Matt. 10) in a manner that is edifying, without casting pearls to swine and giving what is holy to dogs (Matt. 7:6). May your words be seasoned with the salt of knowledge, of faith, and of God's Word in order to extend grace to your listeners. Do so not with mocking, jesting and scoffing at the poor ignorant, but with gravity, maturity, moderation, and fear of God (Col. 4:4; Eph. 4:29-32). Treat the Word of God with all honor and reverence, to shut the mouth of your detractors so that they may be forced to confess that God is in you.

Remember Peter's admonition: "If any man speak, let him speak as the words of God" (1 Pet. 4:11). Do not be rash and vainglorious like so many who want to prate about and taunt the Word of God. They put it in their corrupt and polluted mouths without giving it honor or reverence. They mention it only to babble and mock the poor ignorant. They do not learn from it. They are not edified by it. They do not use it to amend their lives. Keep away from such scoffers. By their senseless speech and scandalous lives, they not only put themselves in danger recklessly, but they also put others in danger. When it is time to confess Christ, they deny and abjure him. Let us heed the apostle who says: "Be not deceived: God is not mocked" (Gal. 6:7). If we must suffer and endure some affliction for the truth, let us make sure that it is not in vain or for a cause that is of no edification, but rather for something that would bring glory to the Lord.

If it is His will that we suffer, let us heed Peter's exhortation. May our lives be holy, that none of us may be troubled and punished "walking in wantonness, lusts, drunkenness, in gluttony, drinkings, and in abominable idolatries" (1 Pet. 4:3). Do not give an opportunity to your opponents to criticize you. For if we suffer from one of our wrongdoings, there is no honor in this, but rather great shame. More than that, we gravely insult God our Father when He is blasphemed and dishonored by us. We are His children, and He should be sanctified and glorified in us; He called us to sanctification to sanctify His holy name. We pray every day: "Hallowed be thy name" (Matt. 6:9; Luke. 11:2). If therefore, by our fault, He is dishonored and vituperated, are we not mocking Him? For we do the opposite of what we wish and pray. And by our actions we demonstrate that we do not want or desire that which we ask of Him. This is a horrible blasphemy. How are Jesus Christ, our sovereign Lord, and His Gospel being honored? What faith and loyalty do we show Him when we take arms against him and forsake Him to follow the banner of Satan, His enemy? We are guilty of this. We betray our own Lord and King when we sin, rejecting the armor of justice to put on the armor of injustice and iniquity, against Paul's teachings (Rom. 6). Let us make sure not to behave in this way, so that the wicked may not be given a chance to attack us. May they only persecute us because we hate vice and love virtue. We seek and pursue the light; they avoid it. We flee the darkness; they pursue it. Let us conduct ourselves so well that they may only hate us because we do not want to be like them and because they cannot bear the light of God which is in us. It reveals all their filth and impurities, just like the sun drives away the darkness and the obscurity of the night (John 3:19-21). As we make sure that we give our enemies no opportunities to attack us, let us not be like those who are so wise that they refuse to suffer for Jesus Christ and His Church.

Jesus Christ wants us to love His Gospel. He does not want us to hide the talents He has given to each of us. But He does not want us to use them for our own profit. Many abuse the knowledge that God has given them. They prefer, unlike Moses, to be great and honored in Egypt than little and lowly in the desert, with the people of God (Heb. 11:24-26). They prefer the riches and the pleasures of Pharaoh's house to the scorn and the thorns of Jesus' Church. They do not mind the Gospel when it does not cause them any trouble or harm. And so, they serve God in such a way that they bend their knee before Baal every day and deny Jesus Christ openly, regardless of what He said: "For whosoever shall be ashamed of me, and of my words among this adulterous and sinful generation, of him shall the Son of man be ashamed also, when he cometh in the glory of his Father with the holy angels" (Mark 8:38). They are not content with dishonoring the Gospel and being a bad example for the simple and ignorant. They dare to judge and condemn the poor innocent who are so strong and steadfast in their faith in Christ that they are ready to put their heads where these lukewarm apostles would refuse or dare to put a finger.

We see how God visits them and punishes them. He does not grant them to suffer for His name. Very often they fall in great misfortunes. They suffer more because of the world to which they devoted their lives than God's servants suffer for their Master (Isa. 29). More than that, these sorry individuals are often completely forsaken and condemned by God (Rom. 1:18-31). They end up blaspheming against Jesus Christ and mocking the Holy Scriptures, rejecting and condemning them as fables and inventions. This is a much more serious punishment. It is to be feared much more than being burned alive a thousand times. Forsaken by God, these people often hurt themselves and kill themselves with their own hand or commit such great offenses that they must die miserably by the hand of the executioners. Yet they do not have the honor to have suffered as witnesses of the truth. Let us guard ourselves against such dangers. Let us not follow such advice and imitate these individuals. Let us run away from sects, wild opinions, and strange doctrines. Let us keep away from dubious, fantastical, impertinent, and presumptuous minds. Let us heed the simplicity of God's Word (Eph. 4; Heb. 13:9; 1 John 4:1). Let us avoid like the plague all those who despise this simplicity of the Scriptures and of the doctrine of the apostles, for they are too subtle. Like alchemists, they seek the quintessence in God's Word. They want to see more clearly and more deeply than Paul who was caught in the third heaven (2 Cor. 12:7-9; Eph. 4:17-19; 1 Thess. 5:1; 1 John 4:4-6).

Let us not be seduced by vain words, like little children, and let us not believe lightly all men, however godly they may look on the outside. Rather, let us test them and see if they are from God or not. Let us stay away from those who seek to lead us off the royal road, which Jesus Christ and his disciples have shown us, and on which they walked. Let us guard ourselves against those who want to make us speak a different language; against those who wish to make us follow a doctrine other than the one God ordered us to follow, which was revealed by His faithful servants. We should not oppose the truth. But as the wise says, he is too careless who believes too quickly. Let us not abuse the grace and the goodness of God. Let us not make of them a veil of iniquity to cover our corruption and give free rein to our unbridled desires. He commands us to control our desires with His Spirit. He commands us to mortify this physical body and put away the old man (Eccles. 5:1-7; Gal. 5; Col. 3:5; Eph. 4:14).

In times of tribulations when we are tempted to sin, we must call upon God at all hours. We must take courage so that we may not become weary, give way under the load and give up the work of God. Let us also remember that we need to invoke Him in times of prosperity not less than in times of adversity, but much more. For it is more difficult to keep a steady course in times of prosperity than in times of adversity and to overcome the temptations that arise on the right and on the left. We find many examples of this in the old people of Israel, who are given to us as an image of human life. We have an example in David who, being at peace, committed adultery and murder. If we have peace, if our lives are easy, free of trouble, free of adversity and persecution, let us not forget the Lord, but let us remember the counsel of the wise. In times of prosperity let us remember the days of anguish and adversity. Let us remember the captivity of Egypt in the land of Canaan. Let us be careful and pray more diligently than ever. Let us not flatter and trust ourselves. Let us not fall asleep in Egypt. Let us not expect any rest (Eccles. 1; Deut. 5; 16; Matt. 26).

ALWAYS BE READY

Let us always be like those who sail at sea. If no wind is blowing now, let us be even more careful and prepared for storms and tribulations (Matt. 24:42, Luke 7; 1 Thess. 5:6). Let us remember the days of Noah and of Lot's wife. Let us fear that when we say "peace, peace," ruin may catch us by surprise, like birds in a net. For when we do not think about it, a mighty wind and a violent storm will rise and stir up and disturb all things. Let us be like the soldiers at war who are always expecting the attack of the enemy. They know they will surprise them, if they can, when they least expect it and when they feel most secure. Let us not be caught off guard while we drink, banquet, and make merry in the manner of Belshazzar, king of Babylon, and the Babylonians (Dan. 5; 1 Pet. 5:8; Eph. 6). We know that we have an enemy who has no loyalty, who never grants us a moment of peace and rest, unless it is to catch us unprepared and surprise us by treason. Therefore, let us be on our guard. Let us not forget the Lord so that we may not provoke Him to anger, as the Israelites did. This would lead Him to send tyrants to punish us. For if we do not want to obey Him, who is our Father, He will send us teachers such as He gave the Israelites: Pharaohs, Philistines, Moabites, Ammonites, Sennacheribs, Nebuchadnezzars, Assyrians and Babylonians. They will correct and chastise us, until He has totally humbled us and taught us to bend our stiff necks under His yoke.

REPENT AND LOVE YOUR ENEMIES

If we are persecuted; if we endure poverty, miseries and other physical calamities or spiritual afflictions, let us recognize first that we are poor sinners who have deserved from God many afflictions which we could not bear. Let us consider that the only remedy we have is to repent truly, confess our sins to God, and pray ardently to ask for His mercy and forgiveness. For we have offended Him. If we suffer false accusations, violence, banishment, imprisonment, fetters and other afflictions, let us not use insult and blaspheme. Let us not curse those who persecute and afflict us, but let us pray for them (Matt. 5:44, Rom. 12:14). Let us not be like the dog that runs after the stone which was thrown at him and chews on it regardless of who threw it. When Isaiah says that Assur, king of Assyria, is the rod of God's wrath and the scourge of His anger, and the Assyrians with him, the same is true of all the other tyrants and persecutors. Therefore, let us not be more foolish than little children. For, however ignorant they may be, still they remember more the one who beats them than the rod. We will not put out the fire with sulfur and oil, and we will not chase away a devil with another devil. What else do we do when we render evil for evil and when we curse and abuse those who harm us, but irritate God more against us? Do we not throw wood, sulfur and oil on the fire in order to increase it? Are we not adding devils to devils? We must throw water on the fire to extinguish it, not oil. We must repel the devil with Jesus Christ, not with Beelzebub (Matt. 12:26-28). We must defeat our enemies, resist their violence with benedictions and prayers, lamentations, tears, and sighs. These are the tears that God has given us. They have such strength and power that they can pierce the sky. Moses and Aaron did not overcome Pharaoh and the Egyptians through imprecations, execrations, maledictions, wrongs and abuses. Rather, they prayed for them when the plagues of God were oppressing them, although they were incredibly hardened and most cruel (Exod. 8; 9).

VENGEANCE IS THE LORD'S

Let the Lord avenge us, He who hears the cries, the sighs, and the lamentations of his servants. He will not let them unavenged. He does not say without reason: beware that your brother and neighbor do not "cry unto the Lord against thee, so that sin be in thee" (Deut. 15:9; 24:15). He heard the cry and saw the tears of the Israelites when they cried to Him (Exod. 3). Let us follow the example of David and of Jesus Christ, who is the epitome of all gentleness and kindness. If we want Him to be our shepherd, let us be His sheep. For He is not the shepherd of the dogs, swine, bears, lions, and foxes, but of the sheep (John 10:2). He prays for those who crucify Him (Luke 23:33-34). Therefore, let us not curse those who afflict us, but let us pray for them with Him. Let us not be angry at them, but at ourselves because we are most often responsible for our own evils. We truly deserve such scourges and punishments from God. Let us remember who we are. When Shimei cursed and persecuted David so outrageously, David said that God has sent those who persecute us to humble us and to try our patience; to let us know our sins and to ask for His mercy so that He may pity us, forgive us, and turn the maledictions of our enemies into benedictions (2 Sam. 16:5-13). Therefore, let all the Shimeis shout. Let us leave them in the hand of God, who will punish them in due time. As for us, let us humble ourselves before the Lord.

If we behave like this, we can be sure that the Lord who is the Lord of hosts, who holds everything in His hand, will deliver us from the violence of our enemies. We will be quiet, and He will fight for us. He will use all the elements and all the creatures for our salvation, and for the ruin and damnation of our enemies. For He will punish them even more severely than we wanted, as can be seen in so many stories and examples of all times. He drowned Pharaoh and his army in the depths of the Red Sea (Exod. 14). He consumed by fire the Babylonians who were around the furnace in which had been thrown the Hebrews (Dan. 3:22). Saul, and several other tyrants, by the just judgment of God, killed themselves with their own sword (I Sam. 31:4). David did not need to pursue him to kill him. For he was avenged beyond his expectations. He did not have to hang Ahithophel (2 Sam. 17:23). Nor did the apostles have to pursue Judas for him to be punished for his evil acts (Matt. 27:5; Acts 1:18). For Ahithophel and Judas punished themselves. Sennacherib's executioners were his own children, and it cost Hezekiah nothing to avenge himself of his tyranny (Isa. 37:38). Herod and Antiochus (Acts. 12:23; 2 Mac. 9:9) grew worms and vermin in their bodies, which consumed and devoured them. The Lord punishes such tyrants every day either through sedition of the people, through war, or some other woes. We have the examples of Ahaz (2

Kings 16) and Ahab (1 Kings 22), Manasseh (2 Kings 21) and Ze-
dekiah (2 Kings 25), and of so many Roman emperors. And when
they had no other punishments than the fears and the frights that
God gave them, they could not be at peace. These same fears were
experienced by Cain, the scribes and Pharisees and the other enemies of Jesus Christ and of His apostles (Matt. 22; Acts 5). For
although the enemies of Jesus Christ and of His disciples refused to
answer to God, yet God scared them. He would make them afraid
that the people would rise against them.

GIVE THANKS TO THE LORD

Let us leave the wicked in God's hand and let us give Him thanks
for such great goodness we receive from Him daily. For even if we
had received no other good from His hand than the fact that He
created us and made us in His image (Gen. 1), when He could have
made us brute animals, or even toads, scorpions, dragons, swine,
dogs, wolves, or some other monsters. Let us consider that we could
never give Him enough thanks, even if we lived one hundred thousand years, and if we did nothing else. How many more blessings
do we owe Him? For He was not pleased with making us such, and
with giving us dominion over all the elements and all the creatures
for our good pleasure. In addition, he gave us His son Jesus Christ,
and He himself in Him, all His inheritance and His kingdom, making us share in His divine nature and in His immortality (John 3;
Rom. 8; Col. 3; 2 Pet. 1).

We should never be ungrateful to Him. Rather we should pray
continually that He would lead and instruct us so that Satan, the
world, and the flesh may not prevent us from reaching this great
happiness, for which He created and prepared us, and for which
He gave us Jesus Christ His Son, of which I pray that through His
grace we may be made partakers.

> If ye be railed upon for the Name of Christ, blessed are ye: for
> the spirit of glory and of God resteth upon you. (1 Pet. 4:14)

May none of you be tormented because he is a murderer, or a thief, or because he covets his neighbor's possessions. But if one of you is persecuted because he is a Christian, let him not be ashamed, but let him glorify God for it.

> Let us run with patience the race that is set before us, look-
> ing unto Jesus the author and finisher of our faith, who for
> the joy that was set before him, endured the cross, and de-
> spised the shame, and is set at the right hand of the throne
> of God. (Heb. 12:1-2)

www.ingramcontent.com/pod-product-compliance
Lightning Source LLC
Chambersburg PA
CBHW030106070426
42448CB00037B/1172